EARTH ROCKS

SEDIMENTARY ROCKS

Richard Spilsbury

WAYLAND

First published in Great Britain in 2016 by Wayland

Editors: Sarah Eason and Tim Cooke
Cover design: Lisa Peacock

Produced for Wayland by Calcium
All rights reserved.
ISBN: 978 1 5263 0199 4
10 9 8 7 6 5 4 3 2 1

Wayland
An imprint of
Hachette Children's Group
Part of Hodder & Stoughton
Carmelite House
50 Victoria Embankment
London EC4Y 0DZ

An Hachette UK Company
www.hachette.co.uk

www.hachettechildrens.co.uk

Picture acknowledgements:

Key: b=bottom, t=top, r=right, l=left, m=middle, bgd=background

Picture credits: Cover: Shutterstock: Scott Prokop; Inside: Dreamstime: Ronald Adcock 7b, Baloncici 27bl, Bcbounders 8, Czalewski 4t, Foster Eubank 6, Labdog 24b, Littleny 4b, Mangroove 22, Matauw 9, Sarah2 18, Sonsam 1, 14t, Zoran Stojkovi 13b, Takepicsforfun 21, Anthony Aneese Totah Jr 12–13, Elena Yakusheva 5, Zrfphoto 23; NASA: 15t; Shutterstock: 27tr, Alexlukin 16, BMJ 14b, TommyBrison 20–21, Catmando 19t, Celiafoto 13t, Kae Deezign 15b, kkymek 24t, Marques 26t, Dudarev Mikhail 17, Paul B. Moore 11, Presniakov Oleksandr 25, Petr Podrouzek 7t, Marcio Jose Bastos Silva 26b, UrbanImages 19b.

CONTENTS

SEDIMENTARY ROCK

Next time you are on a beach, use a spade to dig up some wet sand and put it in a bucket. You will see that the grains of sand form a layer at the bottom of the bucket. Sand is a type of **sediment**. It is made up of tiny pieces of rock. Sedimentary rock is made from layers of sediment that have turned hard.

Sedimentary rocks have different coloured layers.

COMMON ROCK

About three-quarters of the Earth's land surface and most of the ocean floor is covered by sedimentary rock. The rocks differ depending on the types of sediments they contain. For example, sandstone is rock made from billions of sand grains.

LAYERED AND SOFT

Sedimentary rock has many layers and is usually softer than other rocks. There are two other major rock types on the Earth. **Igneous rock** is very hard and is formed from melted **minerals**. **Metamorphic rock** is igneous or sedimentary rock that formed under great heat or **pressure** underground.

Not all sediments are pieces of worn-down rock. Some are parts of shells from dead ocean animals. Others are tiny grains of light ash from **volcanoes**. When volcanoes **erupt**, they shoot out ash, which settles on the ground.

The Cappadocia region in Turkey is famous for its sedimentary rock. Its rock formed from layers of **ash** sediment that was thrown out long ago by a volcano. The rock is so soft that people have even carved homes and churches into it!

ROCK STAR STORIES

homes in Cappadocia

SEDIMENTS ON THE MOVE

Rock is hard and heavy. However, did you know that air and water can move whole mountains of rock and crumble them into pieces?

FROM ROCK TO GRAIN

When water fills a crack during winter, it sometimes freezes into ice in the cold air. Ice takes up more space than water, so it forces the crack to widen a little. Imagine this process happening thousands of times, over thousands of years. This is one example of **weathering**. Huge rocks are reduced to tiny grains during weathering. Rocks also undergo weathering when plant roots grow into them or when wind blows sand against the rock, scratching its surface.

Chunks of eroded rock fall and build up below weathered mountain slopes.

Clues to the Past

Did you know that we eat rock? The salt we put on our food is halite, or rock salt, that has been ground into tiny pieces! It formed when water in ancient seas **evaporated**. During evaporation, the minerals that had **dissolved** in the water turned into solid **salt crystals.**

The Ganges-Brahmaputra River erodes more sediment than any other river. Some of this is rock weathered from the Himalayas. The sediment is washed into the river by streams and rainwater. Each year, the river moves more than 1 billion tonnes of sediment. That is enough sediment to fill all the cargo ships on Earth four times over!

Himalayas

GRAIN TO SEDIMENT

Rushing water in a river, heavy rainfall, pounding waves on a beach or gusts of strong wind can all carry rock grains from one place to another. The process is called **erosion**. When water or wind slows down, the grains of rock they carry fall to the ground or sink underwater.

Moving water carries small rock pieces that weather larger rocks.

LAYING DOWN LAYERS

Over millions of years, layers of sediment turn into layers of sedimentary rock, called **strata**. How does this happen?

Look at the hundreds of strata in this eroded hill of desert sandstone.

PRESS AND STICK

A layer of rock sediment weighs many tonnes, so imagine the weight of tens or hundreds of layers! Under the enormous weight of the rock layers above, the lower layers of sediment are pressed so hard that all the water in the layers is pushed out. Some minerals present in the sediments dissolve in the water, and glue the sediment grains together. This is how sedimentary rock forms. Over many years, as more layers of sediment form on the Earth's surface, more rock is formed in the squashed layers of sediment beneath.

TWISTED AND TURNED

In some places, sedimentary rock has vertical or wavy layers. It did not always look like this, however. Over time, movements in the enormous blocks of rock under the Earth's surface pushed the horizontal strata of sedimentary rock upwards. The rock at the surface also became weathered and eroded. Some of the rock grains even became part of new sedimentary rocks!

In any sedimentary rock, the oldest sediment layers were **deposited** first. They are found at the bottom of the rock. Moving up the rock, the layers become younger and younger. The layer at the surface is the youngest of all. Sedimentary rocks can be different depths, but the deepest can be more than 12 kilometres deep!

strata in desert rock

ROCK STAR STORIES

In the late eighteenth century, a geologist called William Smith became the first person to realise that rock strata stretched all the way across England. He knew this because rock in one place was the same as rock found hundreds of miles away. In 1815, Smith drew the first **geological map** of any country.

THE GRAND CANYON

Perhaps the most incredible view of strata is in the Grand Canyon in Arizona, in the south-western United States. The canyon is 1.6 kilometres deep, 29 kilometres across and 277 kilometres long!

HOW THE GRAND CANYON WAS FORMED

We can view thousands of metres of strata in the Canyon because of the action of one river. The Colorado River formed on top of the highest layer of sedimentary rock in the area that is today the Grand Canyon. Its movement gradually weathered and eroded the rock. Over millions of years, the river cut deeper down through the rock and carried more and more sediment away, leaving an enormous hole: the Grand Canyon!

Clues to the Past

Rocks prove that seas have covered parts of the United States at different times in the past. Around 150 million years ago, most of the area that is now the Rocky Mountains was submerged under a shallow sea. Scientists know this because sedimentary rock containing oyster and squid fossils was found there.

HISTORY OF TIME

The Grand Canyon's strata are a spectacular history timeline. One of the lowest strata is mudstone, which was formed from the floor of an ocean that covered the region more than 500 million years ago. Long after the ocean had dried up, a desert formed on the same spot. The desert is recorded by a sandstone layer higher up in the strata.

the Grand Canyon

ROCK STAR STORIES

Did you know that we cannot see the biggest **canyon** on the Earth? It is found on Greenland and is hidden beneath 3.2 kilometres of ice. Scientists first discovered the canyon in 2013 by using special equipment that can see through the ice. The canyon is almost twice as long as the Grand Canyon and was formed when Greenland was a much warmer place.

FOSSILS IN THE ROCK

Imagine that you are walking on a beach and you spot some sedimentary rock with a strange, shell-shaped pattern. It looks a little like the shells you might find in a rock pool. You have found a **fossil**! A fossil is all that is left of something that lived long, long ago.

TURNING TO STONE

Fossils are the remains of living things that are preserved in rock. Fossils form over millions of years after dead plants or animals become covered with layer upon layer of sediment. The soft parts of plant and animals mostly rot away. However, the tough, hard parts last longer. Minerals in the sediment soak through the hard remains and turn them into stone.

A trilobite is an ancient sea creature.

Some ancient living things did not become complete fossils, but still left traces of their lives in the rocks. These are called trace fossils. They include the tracks left by animals as they walked or ran along the ground. Pieces of feathers or hair that fell from animals as they moved, or leaves that fell from trees and bushes, can all form trace fossils. Even animal droppings and other waste can fossilise. Trace fossils tell us how animals and plants of the distant past lived.

trace fossil dinosaur tracks

ROCK STAR STORIES

In the late 1970s, a fossil hunter called Jack Horner found many fossil nests. The nests had been made by a dinosaur never seen before. Horner named it Maiasaura. The fossils included not only nests and eggs, but also skeletons of babies and even young Maiasaurs. It was proof that the youngsters stayed in the nest for some time after hatching, probably because they were cared for by their parents.

dinosaur eggs

CONGLOMERATES

Conglomerates are **coarse-grained** sedimentary rocks. They formed over thousands of years as sediments were deposited.

conglomerate

WHAT ARE CONGLOMERATES?

Conglomerates are made from large pieces of rounded gravel or pebbles. The edges of the pebbles were rounded when they were picked up by moving water and tossed against other pebbles and rocks. The pebbles or gravel were then dropped onto beaches or in river channels, where they built up into piles of sediment. Over time, the weight of these piles squashed the tiny pieces of sand and clay, and the water, between the pebbles. This formed a kind of cement that stuck the pebbles together.

Buried pebbles can turn into a conglomerate.

Clues to the Past

In September 2012, some conglomerate rock was found on the surface of the planet Mars. The rounded gravel in the conglomerate is evidence that a stream or a beach had moved the rocks and shaped them into rounded pebbles. This proves that water once flowed on Mars!

Mars

USING CONGLOMERATES

Conglomerates do not break cleanly, and because they are made up of different sizes and types of rocks it is hard to know how strong they are until they are tested. This makes them difficult to use. Conglomerates that are only weakly cemented together can be crushed to make **aggregate** for concrete.

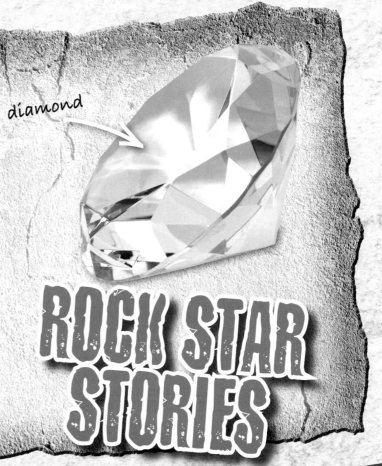

diamond

Certain rocks in conglomerates can be used to find diamonds! Most diamonds are found in an igneous rock called kimberlite. If a conglomerate contains lumps of kimberlite, it tells people that there may be some kimberlite containing diamonds somewhere upstream!

ROCK STAR STORIES

SANDSTONE

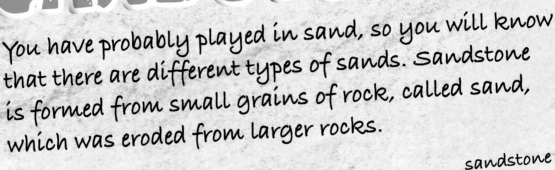

You have probably played in sand, so you will know that there are different types of sands. Sandstone is formed from small grains of rock, called sand, which was eroded from larger rocks.

sandstone

SAND IN THE ROCK

Some rocks form coarse-grained sands and others form fine-grained sands. The appearance of sand also depends on how it has been weathered or eroded. Sand that has sharp, angular grains is often newly-weathered and from hard rocks. Rounded sand grains may have been worn smooth by being eroded in rivers for a long time.

USES OF SANDSTONE

Sandstone is easy to cut and carve but, unlike limestone, it is **resistant** to weathering. For this reason, it is often used for building and to make paving stones. Sandstone is also pretty and comes in different colours, including red, yellow, grey and brown. It is used to make decorative features such as fireplaces, statues and fountains. Sandstone is often ground down and used in concrete, too.

ROCK STAR STORIES

Most sandstone contains quartz grains. Quartz is a common mineral. It is also very hard and tough so is difficult to wear down. Sandstone formed from quartz grains alone is known as quartzite and is very hard.

Clues to the Past

Fossils are often found in sandstone, giving us clues about creatures that once lived in ancient waters. However, sandstone also reveals other things about ancient seas and oceans. Have you seen sand on a beach piled up in ripples or shaped into curved lines by the waves? Sometimes sand becomes buried and hardens into rock with the ripple marks still visible. This reveals the movement of water millions of years ago.

sand ripples

MUDSTONE

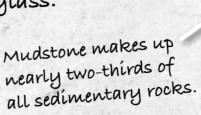

Mudstone is made from ancient mud. The very tiny grains of clay inside this rock are so small that they can be seen only with a magnifying glass.

Mudstone makes up nearly two-thirds of all sedimentary rocks.

MAKING MUDSTONES

Clay is a type of fine-grained soil or mud. Mudstone forms when tiny pieces of clay settle on the bottom of oceans, lakes or even the beds of slow-flowing rivers. Over time, the mud is buried by heavy layers of sediment, which squeeze the water out of the mud and turn it into mudstone. Sometimes, mud, silt and clay are **compressed** into a soft, dark-coloured mudstone called shale.

ROCK STAR STORIES

Oil shale contains substances that can be used to make oil. However, oil from shale is expensive to buy because a lot of energy is needed to **extract** the oil. The rock must be heated to temperatures reaching 538° centigrade in order to release the oil, then the rock is cooled.

The Burgess Shale is a world-famous fossil field that was discovered in the Canadian Rocky Mountains in 1909. The shale here is special because its strata contain tens of thousands of rare fossils. These include many delicate, soft-bodied creatures that date from around 500 million years ago. Before 1909, the remains of such creatures had never been found.

This is how one of the soft-bodied animals found as a fossil in the Burgess Shale may have looked!

Mount Burgess, Rocky Mountains

USING MUDSTONES

High-quality clays or mudstones are used to make pottery. Bricks and roof tiles are also often made from mudstone. Cement is made from crushed mudstone that has been heated and mixed with limestone. Shale splits very easily into thin sheets, so it is used to make floor and roof tiles.

LIMESTONE

Limestone rock is formed from the remains of billions of tiny sea creatures. As the creatures died, their bodies built up on the ocean floor, eventually turning into limestone. This rock can be used for many different things and it is an important resource.

MAKING LIMESTONE

Limestone is mostly formed from the mineral calcite, which is a type of **calcium carbonate**. Sea animals, such as oysters and coral, take in calcite from seawater. Calcite forms bones and shells. When the animals die, the soft parts of their bodies rot away. Their skeletons and shells, which contain calcite, sink to the ocean floor. There, they later turn into limestone.

ROCK STAR STORIES

Chalk is a soft, pale type of very fine-grained limestone. It crumbles easily to a fine powder. In the past, people used chalk lumps to write on slates and ground-up chalk to clean their teeth. Even today, some toothpaste contains chalk.

USING LIMESTONE

Limestone is an important stone used for buildings and statues. The only problem with limestone is that **acids** in rainwater can slowly weather and erode its surface. Limestone is heated to make lime, which is used to create the two most important building materials on the Earth, concrete and steel. Lime is also used to make a type of glass that is added to soil to improve its quality.

the Chalk Pyramids

The pyramids at Giza, Egypt, were built from limestone rock.

Clues to the Past

The amazing Monument Rock formations in Kansas are known as the Chalk Pyramids. Many fossils of creatures with calcium-filled shells have been found there. The fossils show that, 80 million years ago, the area was covered by an ocean teeming with tiny, shelled animals.

UNDERGROUND WORLDS

Limestone is a sedimentary rock that can be dissolved and worn away by rainwater. This creates caves below the Earth's surface. In these underground worlds, rock takes on awesome new forms!

CREATING CAVES

Caves form gradually in underground layers of limestone rock. Rainwater seeps into the ground through cracks in the surface and by soaking into underground rocks. Over time, rainwater dissolves more and more limestone, causing small gaps to widen into big caves. As rainwater weakens layers of limestone, large chunks of it may fall from cave ceilings, making the caves even bigger.

Limestone caves like this one form over thousands of years.

STALACTITES AND STALAGMITES

Limestone caves are not simply empty holes. Remarkable icicle-shaped rocks hang from cave ceilings and rise up from cave floors. These are **stalactites** and **stalagmites**. A stalactite is made when mineral-rich water drips from a cave ceiling. A stalagmite is made when mineral-rich water drips onto the cave floor and builds up into a structure. Sometimes, stalactites and stalagmites grow together to form a pillar that stretches from the ceiling of the cave to its floor.

Stalactites start out as narrow mineral tubes that hang down from cave ceilings. They grow thicker and wider as water trickles down them, depositing more mineral layers on top of the early layers. Scientists can tell how old stalactites are by their width. When a stalactite breaks off, rings inside show the growth history of the stalactite.

Limestone caves full of stalactites and stalagmites are popular tourist attractions in many places around the world. At Carlsbad Caverns in New Mexico, there are spectacular limestone formations on the walls, ceiling and floors!

ROCK STAR STORIES

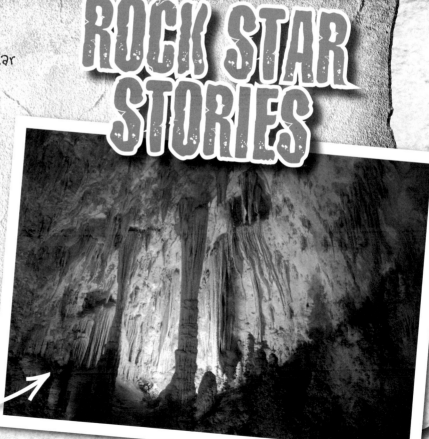

Carlsbad Caverns

SEDIMENTARY POWER

People get most of the energy needed to power machines from **fossil fuels**. These include coal, gas and oil. These fossil fuels are always found between strata in sedimentary rock.

coal

Oil and gas rigs far out at sea extract oil and gas from the seabed.

FOSSIL FUELS

Coal is a hard rock formed from ancient forests that have been buried and squashed by sediment. It is widely used as a fuel in power stations that produce the electricity we need to power our computers and light our homes. Gas and oil are mostly formed from the remains of ocean **plankton** that were trapped among strata. Gas is used in power stations but also to heat homes. Oil is made into petrol and other fuels that power vehicles.

ENERGY PROBLEM

Burning fossil fuels releases a gas, called **carbon dioxide**, into the Earth's atmosphere. Carbon dioxide traps heat from the sun and is causing our planet to become warmer. This **global warming** is melting ice at the Poles and making some places hotter, wetter, drier or stormier than usual.

This is having a huge impact on people, plants and animals around the world. We are also running out of fossil fuels because they take millions of years to form. People are trying to solve this problem by using more **renewable energy**, such as **solar power**, which does not cause global warming and will never run out.

ROCK STAR STORIES

A coal mine in Illinois contains the largest fossil forest ever seen. It covers almost 10 square kilometres and features some individual fossilised plants that measure 10 metres long! Scientists believe the plants were preserved when a whole forest was buried in sediment during an **earthquake** that took place more than 300 million years ago.

fern leaf fossil

Clues to the Past

Some lumps of coal contain fossilised leaves of the plants from which the coal formed. The fossils often look like fern leaves.

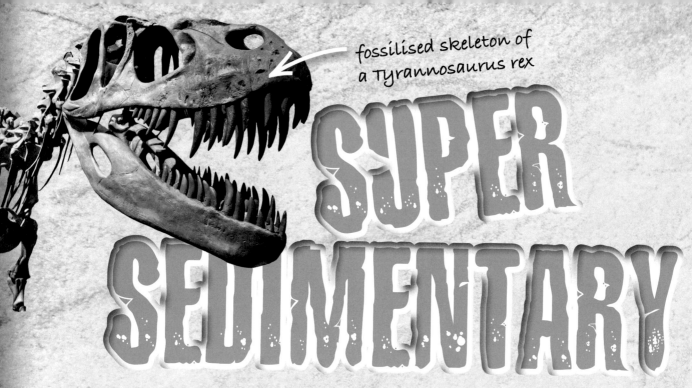
fossilised skeleton of a Tyrannosaurus rex

SUPER SEDIMENTARY

Imagine life without sedimentary rocks. There would be no coal or oil, no concrete and no fossils. Sedimentary rocks form much more slowly and less dramatically than igneous rocks, but they are no less important.

Fossils from the age of the dinosaurs show us how ancient creatures looked.

EARTH-CHANGING ROCKS

The shape of our planet's outer surface is constantly changing because of sedimentary rocks. New layers form as sediments are laid down, and old layers weather and erode. This reveals the fossils that the strata contain, which helps us to learn more about life on the Earth long ago.

Sedimentary rocks are closely linked with all other rocks on the Earth through the **rock cycle**. Igneous rock weathers and erodes into sediment that eventually forms sedimentary rock. Deep layers of sedimentary rock are heated and compressed by powerful underground forces, changing them into metamorphic rock. Extreme heat underground can melt metamorphic rock so that, when volcanoes erupt at the Earth's surface, the rock becomes igneous rock.

Granite is an igneous rock.

Marble is a metamorphic rock.

VITAL RESOURCE

Sedimentary rocks are not only useful for providing us with fossil fuels and building materials. Vital water is stored in the spaces and cracks of some of their layers. The grains of sedimentary rocks such as sandstone can also filter dirt from water, which makes it cleaner. We use this fresh water for watering crops, drinking and for use in factories. Life on the Earth would not be the same without sedimentary rock.

ROCK YOUR WORLD!

It takes thousands of years for sedimentary rock to form, but you can recreate the rock-forming process for yourself!

YOU WILL NEED:

- teaspoon
- sand
- two paper cups
- fine gravel
- water
- sugar
- wax paper or baking parchment
- magnifying glass

paper cup

dried sand and gravel mixture

COMPLETE THESE STEPS:

1. Pour two spoonfuls of sand into a paper cup. Then put two spoonfuls of gravel on top in the same cup. Repeat until you have four layers in total.

2. Put one teaspoon of water into the other cup. Add five spoonfuls of sugar to the water, and stir until the sugar is dissolved.

3. Slowly pour the sugar and water mixture into the cup of sand and gravel. Make sure the sand and gravel are really wet, and then gently pour away any excess water.

4. Leave the wet sand and gravel to dry for one day. Then, carefully cut away the paper cup and tip your 'rock' onto a piece of baking parchment.

5. Leave the rock to harden for at least two days.

6. When it has set solid, look at your rock with a magnifying glass. What can you see?

WHAT HAPPENED?

You made sedimentary rock! Most sedimentary rocks are formed under the water in swamps, lakes, seas and oceans. The sugar in the water acted like the dissolved minerals that make sedimentary rock in nature. The sugar formed a cement that held the sediment (the gravel and sand) together in strata, or layers.

TRY IT OUT!

Create more strata in your sedimentary rock by making it in a wide straw. Rest the bottom end in a bowl. Soak every two layers in sugar solution and let them dry before adding the next two. How many layers can you add? Have they bound together when you cut away the straw?

GLOSSARY

acids Strong substances that can damage objects and structures.

aggregate A material that contains a lot of separate pieces that are squashed together.

ash A powder or dust left behind after something has burnt.

canyon A deep valley with steep sides.

calcium carbonate A type of mineral common in rocks such as limestone and marble, but also in animal shells.

carbon dioxide A gas in the air.

coarse-grained Made up of rough grains.

compressed Squashed.

deposited Dropped somewhere.

dissolved When a solid has broken down into a liquid like water.

earthquake The sudden, violent shaking of the ground.

erosion When pieces of rocks are carried somewhere new by water or wind.

erupt When a volcano explodes and hot, melted rock called lava spurts out of it.

evaporated When a substance has changed from a liquid into a gas.

extract To remove.

fossil The remains or an impression of an ancient plant or animal that is preserved in rock.

fossil fuels Coal, oil and gas fuels formed from the remains of living things that died millions of years ago.

geological map A map showing different geological features, such as the types of rocks found in parts of a country.

global warming The increase in the Earth's temperature, caused partly by people burning fossil fuels such as coal and oil.

igneous rock Rock formed from magma at or below the surface of the Earth.

metamorphic rock Rock that has been changed from its original form by heat and/or pressure.

minerals Solid substances found naturally on the Earth that make up rocks.

plankton Microscopic plants and animals.

pressure To be squashed or squeezed.

renewable energy Energy from a source that will not run out, such as wind or solar power.

resistant Able to resist being affected by something.

rock cycle The process by which rocks of one kind change into rocks of another kind.

salt crystals Solid, regular shapes of salt minerals.

sediment Solid but tiny grains of matter such as sand or silt.

solar power Electricity generated from from the energy of the sun.

stalactites Rocky columns that grow down from a limestone cave ceiling.

stalagmites Rocky columns that grow up from a limestone cave floor.

strata Layers in rock.

volcanoes Openings in the Earth from which hot, melted rock from deep inside the planet bursts out onto its surface.

weathering The wearing away of rock and other substances by wind, water and ice.

FURTHER READING

BOOKS

Callery, Sean, *100 Facts About Rocks and Minerals*, Miles Kelly Publishing, 2009

Dorling Kindersley, *Rock and Mineral*, DK Children, 2014

Green, Dan, *Rocks and Minerals* (Discover More), Scholastic, 2013

Rocks and Minerals Sticker Book, Natural History Museum, 2012

WEBSITES

Learn more about the rock cycle and sedimentary rock at:
www.geolsoc.org.uk/ks3/gsl/education/resources/rockcycle/page3458.html

Watch animations about rock cycle processes such as weathering and erosion at:
www.learner.org/interactives/rockcycle/change3.html

Watch a video about rocks and rock formation at:
www.bbc.co.uk/bitesize/ks3/science/environment_earth_universe/rock_cycle/activity

INDEX

EARTH ROCKS
Titles in the Series

CRYSTALS

978 1 5263 0203 8

Crystals
From the Deep
Solutions
Cave Crystals
Crystal Shape
Crystal Colour and Strength
Finding Earth's Crystals
Mining Crystals
Important Crystals
Precious Stones
Crystals on Demand
Crystals in Crisis
Rock Your World!

IGNEOUS ROCKS

978 1 5263 0205 2

Igneous Rocks
Rocks From Beneath
Birth of Gemstones
Surfacing Rocks
Violent Volcanoes!
Explosive Rocks
Igneous World
Getting Igneous Rocks
Tough Rocks
Versatile Volcanics
Living by Volcanoes
Incredible Igneous
Rock Your World!

METAMORPHIC ROCKS

978 1 5263 0207 6

Metamorphic Rock
Shifting Earth
Underground Rock Factory
Pressure Points
Hot Water
Slate
Marble
Gneiss
Minerals
Reaching the Surface
Metamorphic Worldwide
Amazing Metamorphic
Rock Your World!

MINERALS

978 1 5263 0209 0

Minerals
Rock Minerals
Making Minerals
Space and Water
Recycled Minerals
Types of Minerals
Around the World
Mining Minerals
Useful Minerals
Living Minerals
Mighty Metals
Minerals Matter
Rock Your World!

SEDIMENTARY ROCKS

978 1 5263 0 1994

Sedimentary Rock
Sediments on the Move
Laying Down Layers
The Grand Canyon
Fossils in the Rock
Conglomerates
Sandstone
Mudstone
Limestone
Underground Worlds
Sedimentary Power
Super Sedimentary
Rock Your World!

SOIL

978 1 5263 0 2014

Secret Soil
From Rocks to Soil
Moving Rocks
Sudden Soils
Plants in Soil
Recyclers
Animals in Soil
Different Soils
Soils Around the World
Using Soil
Spoiling Soil
Super Soil
Rock Your World!

WAYLAND
www.waylandbooks.co.uk